551.5   Broekel, Ray.
BRO
          Experiments with
          air.

                              33197000037601
$15.27

DATE			
1-20 3			3-R

A New True Book

EXPERIMENTS
WITH AIR

By Ray Broekel

CHILDRENS PRESS ®

CHICAGO

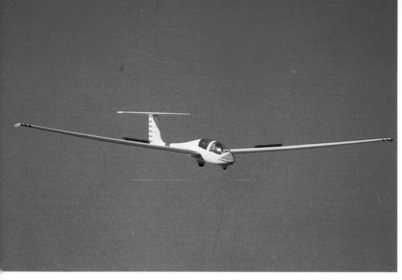

Sailplanes have no engines.
They float on air currents.

PHOTO CREDITS

© Cameramann International, Ltd. — 45

Journalism Services:
© Dave Brown — 40, 42
© Dirk Gallian — 2, 4 (bottom), 44 (top)
© Mike Kidulich — 44 (bottom left)
© Carole Jacobson — 21
© Joseph Jacobson — 4 (top), 7 (2
photos), 9 (2 photos), 11, 12 (2 photos),
14, 22, 27 (2 photos), 30, 31 (2 photos),
34, 36, 37 (2 photos), 38, 39, 44
(bottom right)
© John Patsch — Cover, 10, 16, 17, 19 (2
photos), 21 (2 photos), 23 (2 photos), 25,
29, 32 (2 photos)

Cover: Air temperature is cooler near the
floor

For Ruby

Library of Congress Cataloging-in-Publication Data

Broekel, Ray.
  Experiments with air.

  (A New true book)
  Includes index.
  Summary: Presents experiments which demonstrate
the properties of air.
    1. Air—Experiments—Juvenile literature. [1. Air
—Experiments. 2. Experiments] I. Title.
QC161.2.B76 1988   551.5   87-34146
ISBN 0-516-01213-4

Childrens Press®, Chicago
    3 4 5 6 7 8 9 10 R 97 96 95 94 93 92 91 90 89

TABLE OF CONTENTS

Flags waving and clothes drying are examples of moving air at work.

WHAT IS AIR?

Air is all around us. You cannot see it, but you can see what it does. A flag on a flagpole is blown by moving air. Moving air is called wind. You can feel wind on your skin.

Is a glass empty when it has no water in it? Of course not. The glass is filled with air. The air takes up space in the glass.

Air takes up space that is not filled by other things. Air is a mixture of invisible gases that form the atmosphere of the earth.

These gases are mostly oxygen, nitrogen, carbon dioxide, and hydrogen.

You can prove that a glass is filled with air. Do the following experiment.

EXPERIMENT

Equipment:
paper napkin
glass
aquarium filled with water

This experiment shows that air takes up space.

Press a crumpled paper napkin firmly into the bottom of the glass. Then carefully put the glass, mouth down, into the water until the mouth touches the bottom. Do not tilt the glass.

Remove the glass slowly. Take out the crumpled paper napkin.

Is it wet or dry? It is dry. Do you know why? The air in the glass kept the water out and so the paper napkin is dry.

Whoever heard of pouring a glass of air? You can do it!

EXPERIMENT

Equipment:
2 glasses
aquarium filled with water

Put one glass into the aquarium and let it fill with water. Now push the second glass into the water, mouth down. Do not let water get into it as you set it down on the bottom.

Raise the water-filled glass above the glass with air in it. Tilt the glass with air in it to allow air bubbles to escape. Allow the bubbles to go into the water-filled glass. Watch closely. The air bubbles will push the water right out of the glass!

You have proved again that air is real. It takes up space. And it can be poured from one glass into another.

This experiment shows how air bubbles push water out of a glass.

Air can support weight.

EXPERIMENT

Equipment:
paper bag
book

Blow up a paper bag and close the end. Now place the bag on a table. Put a book on the bag. What holds up the book? How does this experiment show you that air is real?

Air has no shape of its own, so it takes on the shape of the object that contains it. But air is real, and can support the weight of objects placed on it.

In what other ways is air used to hold up things? What about a bicycle tire? An automobile tire? A basketball?

AIR MOVES

You cannot see air, but you can feel it when it moves.

Have you ever fanned your face or stood in front of an electric fan? You were feeling moving air, or wind.

You can feel air.
Smoke must move in
the direction the
wind is moving.

12

You can see the effects of air moving. If there is a strong wind, trees will sway. Flags and smoke will be blown in the direction the wind is moving.

EXPERIMENT

Blow onto the back of your hand, holding your hand close to your mouth. What do you feel?

What have you done? What proof is this that air is a real thing?

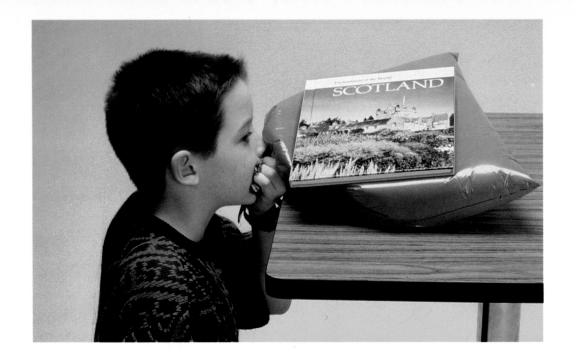

EXPERIMENT

Equipment:
plastic bag
table
book

Place an empty big plastic bag, on the table. Let the opening hang over the edge of the table. Place a book on the flattened part of the bag.

Now blow into the bag. As you fill the bag with air, what happens to the book? What makes the book rise?

AIR IS EVERYWHERE

It is around your body. It is in the soil. It is even in solid things. Try these experiments.

EXPERIMENT

1. Run down the sidewalk. What happens to the air as you run? Your body pushes the air aside. So you really don't notice that the air is there.
   Now take a big sheet of cardboard and hold it in front of you as you race down the same sidewalk. What happens to your speed? You are slowed down. Why? The cardboard slows you down as the air pushes against it!

Experiment with soil
in a glass of water.
What do you see?

Equipment:
soil
glass
water

2. Take a handful of soil and place it in
    a glass. The soil should make a layer
    about two inches thick. Then fill the
    glass with water.
      Let the glass sit for about an hour.
    Then watch it. What do you see?
    Bubbles of air rise from the soil through
    the water. This proves that air is present

Will the brick in water give off air bubbles?

in the soil. Bits of air fill the spaces
between the bits of soil. This air rises
through the glass of water in the form
of air bubbles. Air is everywhere.

Equipment:
brick   aquarium   water

3. Air is found in solid things, too. Take
a brick and place it in an aquarium
filled with water. Let the brick sit for an
hour or so. Then observe what happens.
    Do you see the air bubbles? Where is
the air coming from?

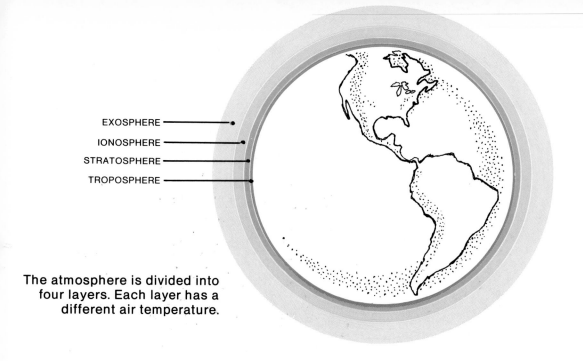

EXOSPHERE

IONOSPHERE

STRATOSPHERE

TROPOSPHERE

The atmosphere is divided into four layers. Each layer has a different air temperature.

AIR HAS WEIGHT

The earth is surrounded by air that is about five hundred miles deep. Even though you cannot see it, this air has weight. You can prove air has weight by doing these experiments.

You can weigh air in a basketball.

EXPERIMENT

Equipment:
basketball (flat)   air pump   scale

1. Weigh the empty basketball on the
    scale.
    Then pump the basketball full of air
    with the air pump. Now weigh the ball
    again.
    What happened? The weight has
    increased. What caused this to happen?
    The air that was pumped into the
    basketball has weight. It showed up on
    the scale.

19

How does this experiment prove that air has weight?

Equipment:
2 balloons   string   thumbtack   yardstick

2. Place the thumbtack at the top of a door frame. Now tie one end of a long piece of string to the thumbtack and then to the center of the yardstick.

Blow up the two balloons and tie their ends with string. Tie the other ends of the string to the ends of the yardstick.

The two balloons should be balanced on the yardstick. Now prick one of the balloons with the pin. What happens? How have you proved that air has weight?

WARM AIR RISES

When air warms up, it rises. This is because air gets lighter as it gets warmer. You can prove this fact by doing the following experiments.

Heat makes air rise.

EXPERIMENTS

Equipment:
stick   string   sheet of paper   scissors

1. Cut a spiral ribbon out of a sheet of
    paper. Use the string to attach the spiral
    ribbon to the stick. Now hang it over a
    radiator that is giving off heat.
    The rising hot air will make the spiral
    ribbon go around. You have proved that
    warm air rises.

How does this experiment prove that hot air rises?

Equipment: room thermometer   stepladder

2. Place the thermometer on the floor and take the room temperature. Hold the thermometer in position for a minute before taking the reading.

Then stand up and hold the thermometer about four feet above the floor. Wait a minute, then read the thermometer.

Now climb up about three steps on the ladder. Wait a minute and read the thermometer again. What did you discover? Where is the colder air? Where is the warmer air?

AIR HAS PRESSURE

The five hundred miles
of air surrounding the
earth presses about 14.7
pounds on each square
inch of surface. We don't
feel the weight of air
because we are used to it.

EXPERIMENT

Equipment: library books

Have someone place a pile of books on your hand. The books are heavy. They exert pressure on your hand. Now remove the books. What about the air? Do you feel the pressure of it on your hand? No, because you are used to having air all around you, so it just feels natural. But you can really feel the pressure and forces of air when you are walking or running into a strong wind.

When things fall, the air presses on all sides of the object. Prove it by experimenting with a parachute.

EXPERIMENTS

Equipment:

handkerchief	string (2 yards)
tape	spool

1. Do this experiment outside or in a room with a high ceiling.

   Tie one corner of the hankerchief with the end of one piece of string. Now tie the corner next to it with the other end of the string. Do the same with the other half of the handkerchief. Place the spool between the two loops of string. Tape down the string so it doesn't come loose.

   Now fold the handkerchief and throw it up into the air. The handkerchief should billow out and fall to the ground slowly.

What happens when the parachute drops?

Air has weight. Therefore, air also has pressure. The air pressed down on the parachute causing it to fall. Air also presses up inside the parachute to slow it down as it falls.

By doing this experiment you have proved that air presses on all sides of a falling object. You have also proved that air has weight and pressure.

Air causes, or exerts, pressure even when it is not moving.

EXPERIMENTS

Equipment:
thin lightweight stick
newspaper

1. Lay the stick on a table with about
    eight inches sticking over the table
    edge. Cover the part of the stick on the
    table with the three sheets of
    newspaper, smoothing out the sheets to
    make them as flat as possible.

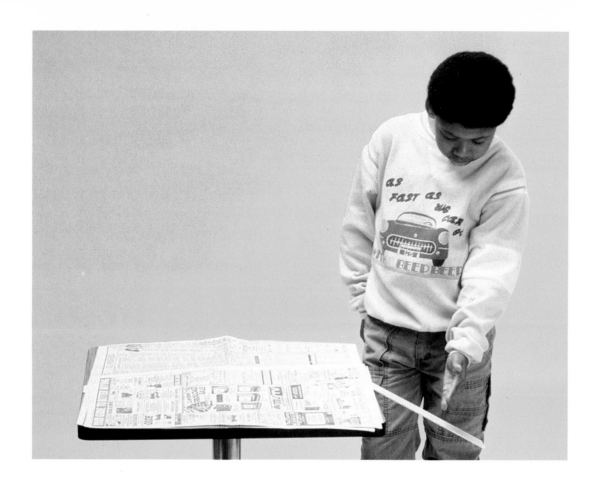

Now strike the piece of wood
extending beyond the table. Do this
quickly and sharply. The stick will break
off. Why? The air pressure on top of
sheets of newspaper is pushing down on
the wood underneath. Instead of flipping
over, the wood breaks into two pieces.
This shows that air can really press
down with force.

Equipment: funnel   Ping-Pong ball

2. Place the ball in the funnel and try to
move it out of the funnel by blowing.
You will find that it is very hard to move
the ball more than a fraction of an inch.
Why is this? Air in motion exerts less
side pressure than still air. Therefore, the
air blowing past the ball will exert less
pressure than the air on top. So the
harder you blow, the less you can move
the ball, as you are simply making the
pressure on top of the ball press down
harder.

Equipment: glass   3x5 index card   water

3. Moisten the index card. Fill the glass
with water. Then put the moistened card

over the opening of the glass. Hold the card in place with one hand, making sure it is flat.

Holding your hand against the card, quickly turn the glass upside down. Now take your hand away. What happens?

Why doesn't the water fall from the glass? What have you proved? You have proved that air presses against things from all sides. Since there was no pressure on the water to fall out, the index card held it in place. This experiment may seem impossible, but it really does work.

Amaze your friends with this experiment with air pressure.

Equipment: can nail hammer

4. Do this air pressure experiment at a sink. Ask an adult to help you make a hole with the nail near the bottom of the can.

Fill the can with water at the sink. Immediately place the palm of one hand tightly over the top of the can. When you do this the water will stop running out of the hole. Why?

Now remove your hand from the top of the can. Why does the water again start running from the hole?

Water runs out of the can on the right but not from the can on the left. Do you know why?

WHAT IS A JET OF AIR?

You can find out for yourself what a jet of air is. Try these experiments with a balloon.

EXPERIMENTS

1. Blow up a balloon. Keep the opening tightly closed so no air can escape.
    Now, keeping your face near the opening, slowly let the air out of the balloon. The air you feel is a jet. The word jet is also used to describe a kind of airplane.

When air rushes out, the balloon moves
away from the moving air.

2. How does a jet plane move? Blow up
   your balloon. Then close the open end
   with your fingers. Let go. What happens?
   Now place a blown-up balloon on the
   edge of a table or a desk. Be sure the
   open end is facing off the table. Now
   remove your fingers. What happens? The
   balloon moves off the table with a
   whoosh!

   The balloon moves in the opposite
   direction of the jet of air. The jet of air
   that comes out is called the exhaust.

   That is the way a jet plane works. The
   engine exhaust goes one way, and the
   plane goes in the other direction.

FUN WITH AIR

Experiments prove facts about air. And some of those experiments can be used as "magic" tricks to surprise your friends.

EXPERIMENTS

Equipment: bottle   candle

1. You can pretend to blow air through a bottle. You will need a bottle and a lighted candle to do this experiment/ trick. Ask an adult to light the candle for you.

Place the lighted candle behind the bottle and blow on the bottle. Your breath seems to pass through the bottle to blow out the flame! Adjust the distance of the candle and bottle to get the best effect.

What happens is that your breath goes around the bottle. The two streams of air come together on the opposite side to blow out the flame.

Equipment: playing cards   bowl

2. Challenge a friend to stand on a chair and drop a card into a bowl on the floor. Unless your friend knows the

This card trick demostrates scientific facts about air.

secret of how to hold the card, the card will miss the bowl. But if you hold the card flat as shown above right, it will fall into the bowl nearly every time.

Why is this? When you drop the card edge first, its slight curvature causes it to curve through the air and land outside the bowl. But the flat card falls straight down. The air resistance below makes it fall more slowly. Practice this trick before trying it out on a friend.

MAKING SOUND WITH AIR

You and your friends can make sound with air. You can make a musical instrument out of a paper straw and air. Try this.

EXPERIMENT

Flatten 1/2 inch of one end of the straw. Then cut off about 1/2 inch from each corner. To play your instrument, insert 1-1/2 inches into your mouth, then close your lips and blow hard. You should get a loud, strong sound.

Flatten the end of a straw

You can raise the pitch of the straw by cutting off pieces of the outer end. Cut straws to different lengths. You can play a different note on each. Then you and your friends can play tunes by taking turns playing different notes.

What you have done is to make a simplified version of a clarinet. Air you blow causes the cut flaps on the straw to flutter. The fluttering, in turn, causes the air column in the straw to vibrate to make the sound you hear.

Although Monument Valley in northern Arizona
looks empty, we know it is full of air.

THINGS TO REMEMBER

You cannot see air, but it is all around you. Air takes up space not taken up by other things. It is a mixture of gases. These gases form the atmosphere of the earth.

Modern windmills are used to generate electrical
power in this plant near Palm Springs, California.

You can feel air as it
pushes against you.
Moving air is called wind.
You know air is there
when it moves.

Air is found in solid things. The air fills spaces not filled by solid matter.

Air has weight. Warm air is lighter than cold air, so it rises. When the air is put under pressure it weighs even more.

The air around the earth is about five hundred miles deep. Air exerts a pressure of about 14.7 pounds on each square inch of surface of the

All living things die without air.

earth. Air exerts pressure
on all sides of an object.

A jet of air coming out
of an object causes the
object to move in the
other direction. Air is
invisible, but it affects all
living things. It cannot be
ignored.

WORDS YOU SHOULD KNOW

air(AYR)—made up of invisible gases
air pressure(AYR PRESH • er)—about 14.7 pounds per square inch at the earth's surface
atmosphere(AT • muss • feer)—the gases that surround the earth
gas(GAS)—a substance that is not solid or liquid but that can expand and move about to fill empty spaces
jet(JET)—a forceful stream of air
pressure(PRESH • er)—the force pushing against a surface
weight(WATE)—the heaviness of a thing
wind(WIND)—moving air

INDEX

About the author

Ray Broekel has been writing children's books for over thirty years. He's written almost a book a year for Childrens Press. Dr. Broekel is well known in the publishing field as a teacher, editor, and author of science materials for young people.

    A full-time freelance writer, Dr. Broekel has written many other kinds of books for both children and adults. He now has almost 200 published books to his credit. He is considered to be the #1 authority on candy bar and chocolate history, having written several books on the subjects. He and his wife, Peg, live with their dog, Fergus, in Ipswich, Massachusetts.